Unlocking the Potential

REAL ESTATE INVESTMENTS

Exploring Opportunities for Wealth Creation

Robert A. Eastsun
2023

About Book

Book Title: Unlocking the Potential: Real Estate
Investments

Sub-title: Exploring Opportunities for Wealth
Creation

Series: 2 of: FROM GRAND TO A MILLION

Type: Digital E-Book

Format: PDF

Size: 6X9 inches - 15.24X22.89 cm

Total Pages: 93

CONTENTS

Preface

Welcome to "From a Grand to a Million: The Secrets to Building Wealth." Series of 2. Book; "Unlocking the Potential: Real Estate Investments".

This book is a result of years of research, experience, and a burning desire to help individuals like you achieve financial success. If you've ever wondered how to turn a modest sum of money into a seven-figure fortune, this book is your roadmap to making it happen.

In today's world, building wealth is not just reserved for the privileged few. With the right knowledge, strategies, and a dash of boldness, anyone can embark on a journey towards financial independence and security. This book aims to empower you with the tools and insights needed to navigate the complex world of investments and make your money work for you.

Welcome to the world of real estate investments, where opportunities for wealth creation abound. In this book, we embark on a journey that delves deep into the dynamic realm of real estate, unveiling its potential as a powerful vehicle for financial growth and independence.

Real estate investments offer a unique pathway to building wealth, with various avenues ranging from residential properties to commercial ventures. Throughout these pages, we aim to equip you with the knowledge and insights needed to navigate this lucrative landscape with confidence.

As we explore the diverse facets of real estate investments, we will analyze market trends, discuss risk management strategies, and explore techniques for maximizing returns. By the end of this journey, you will have gained a comprehensive understanding of the real estate market and its potential to unlock the doors to financial prosperity.

Whether you are a seasoned investor looking to diversify your portfolio or a newcomer seeking to venture into the world of real estate, this book is designed to empower you with the tools necessary to make informed decisions and embark on a journey towards unlocking the true potential of real estate investments. Let's begin this transformative exploration together.

Introduction

Welcome to "Unlocking the Potential: Real Estate Investments," the second book in our series, "From a Grand to a Million: The Secrets to Building Wealth." In this installment, we embark on a thrilling exploration of the dynamic world of real estate investments and unveil the secrets that can propel you towards financial success.

As we delve deeper into the realm of wealth creation, we recognize that real estate investments offer unparalleled opportunities for building and preserving wealth. From residential properties to commercial ventures, the real estate market presents diverse avenues to grow your assets and secure a prosperous future.

In the first book of our series, we established the foundation for understanding the principles of wealth creation, guiding you on how to multiply a modest sum into significant capital. Now, we take the next stride, focusing our attention on the tangible assets and lucrative possibilities that real estate investments offer.

Throughout this book, we will explore the intricacies of the real estate market, examine current trends, and uncover strategies that have the potential to unlock the full scope of opportunities in this field. Whether you are a seasoned investor looking to expand your portfolio or a novice seeking to take your first steps into the world of real estate, our aim is to equip you with the knowledge and tools necessary to make informed decisions.

We recognize that real estate investments can be both exhilarating and challenging. Therefore, we emphasize the significance of diligent research, risk management, and the ability to seize advantageous opportunities. As we progress through these pages, you will learn how to identify lucrative properties, negotiate effectively, and optimize your returns.

Ultimately, building wealth through real estate is not just about monetary gain. It is about creating a stable foundation for financial freedom, security, and a prosperous future for you and your loved ones. By applying the insights shared in this book, you will be well-prepared to navigate the ever-evolving landscape of real estate investments and open the doors to a realm of untapped potential.

So, let's embark on this transformative journey together as we explore the secrets of real estate investments and empower you to unlock the full potential of your wealth-building endeavors. Remember, with dedication, knowledge, and strategic action, you have the power to turn your aspirations into reality. Let's unlock the potential of real estate investments and build a path to enduring prosperity!

Author

Real Estate Investments

Unlocking the Potential: Real Estate Investments

Exploring Opportunities for Wealth Creation

Overview:
In this book, we delve into the world of real estate investments and uncover the potential for wealth creation. From residential properties to commercial ventures, we explore various aspects of real estate investments and provide insights into strategies for success. Discover how you can leverage the power of real estate to grow your wealth and achieve financial independence.

Section 1: Residential Real Estate Investments

1.1 Understanding Residential Real Estate

Residential real estate is a popular and accessible avenue for real estate investments. In this section, we will delve into the fundamentals of residential real estate investments, including its dynamics and factors to consider when entering this market.

1.1.1 Exploring the Residential Real Estate Market
Residential real estate encompasses a wide range of properties, from single-family homes to

condominiums and multi-family units. Understanding the dynamics of the residential market is essential for making informed investment decisions. We will explore the current state of the market, including supply and demand factors, pricing trends, and regional variations.

1.1.2 Types of Residential Properties Different types of residential properties offer unique investment opportunities. We will discuss the characteristics and considerations of various residential property types, such as single-family homes, townhouses, condominiums, and multi-family units. Each type has its own advantages and considerations, and understanding these nuances will help you make informed investment choices.

1.1.3 Factors to Consider When Investing in Residential Properties Successful residential real estate investments require careful evaluation of various factors. We will discuss key considerations such as location, neighborhood dynamics, property condition, rental demand, and potential for future appreciation. Additionally, we will explore the importance of conducting thorough due diligence, including property inspections, market research, and financial analysis, to assess the viability of residential investments.

1.1.4 Financing Residential Investments

Financing plays a crucial role in residential real estate investments. We will explore various financing options available for residential properties, including traditional mortgage loans, government-backed loans, private financing, and creative financing strategies. Understanding the financing landscape and selecting the right financing option can significantly impact your investment returns.

1.1.5 Rental Income vs. Property Appreciation

Residential real estate investments can generate returns through both rental income and property appreciation. We will discuss the advantages and considerations of each approach, including rental market dynamics, property management considerations, and long-term wealth creation potential. Understanding the balance between rental income and property appreciation will help you formulate an investment strategy aligned with your goals.

By gaining a comprehensive understanding of residential real estate investments, you will be equipped with the knowledge and insights to make informed investment decisions in this lucrative sector. Whether you are a first-time investor or looking to expand your real estate portfolio, this section will provide valuable insights into residential real estate investments.

Exploring the residential real estate market and its dynamics

The residential real estate market is a dynamic sector that offers numerous investment opportunities. Understanding its dynamics is essential for navigating this market effectively. In this section, we will explore the residential real estate market in detail, shedding light on key aspects such as market trends, supply and demand dynamics, and factors influencing the housing market.

1. Market Trends: We will examine the current trends in the residential real estate market, including factors like housing inventory levels, home prices, and market competitiveness. Understanding these trends will help investors identify potential opportunities and make informed decisions.

2. Supply and Demand: The balance between housing supply and demand has a significant impact on the residential real estate market. We will analyze factors that affect supply, such as new construction, zoning regulations, and population growth, as well as demand drivers like job markets, demographics, and lifestyle preferences.

3. Regional Variations: The residential real estate market can vary greatly from one region to another. We will explore regional variations in terms of market conditions, pricing trends, and investment potential. By understanding these regional nuances, investors can tailor their strategies to specific markets.

4. Economic Factors: The overall economic environment plays a crucial role in the residential real estate market. We will examine economic indicators, such as interest rates, employment rates, and GDP growth, and discuss how they influence the demand for housing and the overall health of the market.

5. Market Influencers: Several factors influence the residential real estate market, including government policies, demographic shifts, and technological advancements. We will explore how these influencers shape the market landscape and present both challenges and opportunities for investors.

By exploring the residential real estate market and its dynamics, investors can gain valuable insights into the trends, supply and demand dynamics, regional variations, economic factors, and market influencers that drive this sector. Armed with this knowledge, investors can make informed decisions and seize opportunities in the residential real estate market.

Different types of residential properties: single-family homes, condos, multi-family units

Residential real estate offers a variety of property types to suit different investment preferences and objectives. Understanding the characteristics of each property type is crucial when considering residential real estate investments. Here, we explore the three primary types: single-family homes, condos, and multi-family units.

1. Single-Family Homes: Single-family homes are standalone properties designed to accommodate one family. These properties offer privacy, space, and often come with a yard or outdoor area. Investors can choose between buying and renting out single-family homes or purchasing properties for potential resale value.

2. Condos: Condos, short for condominiums, are individual units within a larger residential complex. Condos typically feature shared amenities, such as gyms, swimming pools, and common areas. Investors can purchase condos as rental properties or for personal use, enjoying the convenience of maintenance and management provided by the condo association.

3. Multi-Family Units: Multi-family units consist of properties that can accommodate multiple

families in separate units, such as duplexes, triplexes, or apartment buildings. These properties offer the potential for higher rental income by renting out multiple units simultaneously.

Investors should carefully consider factors such as location, market demand, potential rental income, and property management when evaluating the suitability of each residential property type. Each type has its own advantages and considerations, and understanding these distinctions is essential for making informed investment decisions in the residential real estate market.

Factors to consider when investing in residential properties

Investing in residential properties requires careful consideration of various factors to ensure a successful investment strategy. Here are some key factors to keep in mind when evaluating residential properties:

1. Location: The location of a property plays a significant role in its desirability and potential for appreciation. Consider factors such as neighborhood safety, proximity to amenities, schools, transportation, and job centers.

2. Market Conditions: Analyze the local real estate market, including supply and demand dynamics, pricing trends, and market competitiveness. Understanding market conditions will help you assess the potential for rental income and property appreciation.

3. Property Condition: Evaluate the condition of the property, including its structural integrity, maintenance requirements, and potential renovation costs. A thorough inspection will help identify any potential issues or hidden expenses.

4. Rental Demand: Consider the rental demand in the area. Research rental rates, vacancy rates, and tenant preferences to determine the income potential of the property.

5. Financing Options: Explore different financing options available for residential properties. Evaluate mortgage rates, down payment requirements, and loan terms to assess the financial feasibility of the investment.

6. Property Management: If you plan to rent out the property, consider the responsibilities and costs associated with property management. Determine if you will manage the property yourself or hire a professional management company.

7. Cash Flow Analysis: Conduct a comprehensive cash flow analysis to assess the investment's profitability. Consider all expenses, including mortgage payments, property taxes, insurance, maintenance costs, and potential rental income.

8. Future Development: Research any upcoming development projects or infrastructure improvements in the area. These factors can significantly impact property values and rental demand in the long run.

By considering these factors, investors can make informed decisions and select residential properties that align with their investment goals and risk tolerance. Conducting thorough due diligence is crucial to mitigate risks and maximize the potential returns on residential real estate investments.

1.2 Financing Residential Investments

Financing plays a crucial role in residential real estate investments, as it provides the means to acquire properties and maximize investment potential. In this section, we will explore various financing options available for residential investments and discuss key considerations when securing funding.

1.2.1 Traditional Mortgage Loans: Traditional mortgage loans are a common financing option for residential properties. We will delve into the application process, loan terms, interest rates, and down payment requirements associated with traditional mortgages.

1.2.2 Government-Backed Loans: Government-backed loans, such as those offered by the Federal Housing Administration (FHA) or the Veterans Affairs (VA), provide attractive financing options for qualified borrowers. We will explore the eligibility criteria, benefits, and considerations of government-backed loans.

1.2.3 Private Financing: Private financing involves obtaining funding from individuals or private lending institutions. We will discuss the advantages and considerations of private financing, including potential flexibility in terms and eligibility requirements.

1.2.4 Creative Financing Strategies: Creative financing strategies, such as seller financing, lease options, or partnerships, offer alternative approaches to finance residential investments. We will explore these strategies, highlighting their benefits and potential risks.

1.2.5 Credit and Financial Considerations: Maintaining good credit and financial health is essential when seeking financing for residential investments. We will discuss key factors that lenders consider, including credit scores, income stability, debt-to-income ratios, and reserves.

Understanding the financing options available and evaluating their suitability for your investment goals is crucial for successful residential real estate investments. By exploring traditional mortgages, government-backed loans, private financing, and creative strategies, investors can select the financing approach that aligns with their financial situation and investment objectives.

Financing options for residential real estate investments

When investing in residential real estate, there are various financing options available to help fund the purchase. Here are some common financing options to consider:

1. Traditional Mortgage Loans: Traditional mortgage loans are offered by banks and financial institutions. They involve borrowing a specific amount of money to purchase a property and repaying it over a set term with interest.

2. Government-Backed Loans: Government-backed loans, such as those insured by the Federal Housing Administration (FHA) or guaranteed by

the Veterans Affairs (VA), offer favorable terms and lower down payment requirements for eligible borrowers.

3. Private Financing: Private financing involves obtaining funding from individuals or private lending institutions. This option may offer more flexibility in terms and requirements compared to traditional lenders.

4. Home Equity Loans or Lines of Credit: If you already own a property, you can leverage the equity in your home through a home equity loan or line of credit. This allows you to access funds based on the value of your property.

5. Hard Money Loans: Hard money loans are typically short-term loans provided by private lenders or investors. They are based on the value of the property rather than the borrower's creditworthiness.

6. Crowdfunding: Crowdfunding platforms allow multiple investors to pool their funds to finance real estate projects. This option provides opportunities to invest in residential properties with smaller individual contributions.

7. Seller Financing: In some cases, sellers may offer financing options where they act as the lender and hold a mortgage on the property. This can be

advantageous for buyers who may not qualify for traditional financing.

It's important to evaluate each financing option carefully, considering factors such as interest rates, terms, fees, and eligibility requirements. By understanding the available financing options, investors can choose the one that best suits their financial situation and investment goals when venturing into residential real estate investments.

Understanding mortgage loans, down payments, and interest rates

When financing a residential real estate investment, it's important to understand key concepts such as mortgage loans, down payments, and interest rates. Let's explore each of these elements:

1. Mortgage Loans: A mortgage loan is a financial instrument that allows individuals to borrow money from a lender to purchase a property. The borrower agrees to repay the loan, typically over a set term, through regular payments that include both principal and interest.

2. Down Payments: A down payment is the initial upfront payment made by the buyer towards the purchase price of the property. It is usually

expressed as a percentage of the property's total value. A larger down payment reduces the amount borrowed and can lead to lower interest rates and monthly mortgage payments.

3. Interest Rates: Interest rates represent the cost of borrowing money and are expressed as a percentage. They determine the amount of interest that will be paid over the life of the loan. Interest rates can be fixed (remain constant throughout the loan term) or adjustable (may fluctuate over time).

Understanding mortgage loans, down payments, and interest rates is essential for making informed decisions when financing a residential real estate investment. By familiarizing yourself with these concepts, you can assess affordability, compare loan options, and negotiate favorable terms that align with your financial goals.

Evaluating the financial viability of residential investments

Assessing the financial viability of residential investments is crucial to make informed investment decisions. Here are key factors to consider when evaluating the financial potential of residential properties:

1. Cash Flow Analysis: Analyze the potential rental income and expenses associated with the property. Consider factors such as mortgage payments, property taxes, insurance, maintenance costs, vacancy rates, and property management fees. A positive cash flow indicates a potentially profitable investment.

2. Return on Investment (ROI): Calculate the ROI by comparing the expected income generated from the property (rental income, potential appreciation) with the total investment (purchase price, closing costs, renovation expenses). A higher ROI indicates a more favorable investment opportunity.

3. Market Analysis: Assess the local real estate market conditions, including supply and demand dynamics, rental market trends, and property appreciation rates. This analysis helps determine the potential for property value growth and rental demand.

4. Financing Costs: Consider the interest rate, loan terms, and financing fees associated with acquiring the property. Evaluate the impact of these costs on the overall investment returns.

5. Risk Assessment: Identify and evaluate potential risks such as market volatility, economic conditions, property location, and regulatory changes. Mitigating risks through thorough due

diligence and risk management strategies is essential.

6. Long-Term Potential: Consider the long-term potential for the property in terms of rental income growth, property value appreciation, and future development plans in the area.

7. Exit Strategy: Have a clear exit strategy in mind, whether it involves selling the property at a profit, refinancing, or holding it for long-term rental income.

By carefully evaluating the financial viability of residential investments, investors can make informed decisions and select properties that align with their investment goals and risk tolerance. Conducting thorough financial analysis and considering market factors will contribute to successful residential real estate investment outcomes.

1.3 Strategies for Profitable Residential Investments

To maximize profitability in residential real estate investments, it's essential to implement effective strategies. Here are some strategies to consider:

1. Location Analysis: Focus on properties in desirable locations with strong market fundamentals, such as good schools, amenities, proximity to transportation, and potential for future development.

2. Renovation and Value-Add: Identify properties that have renovation or value-add potential. By improving the property's condition or adding amenities, you can increase its value and rental income potential.

3. Rental Market Research: Conduct thorough research on the local rental market to understand tenant preferences, demand, and rental rates. This helps in setting competitive rental prices and minimizing vacancy periods.

4. Property Management: Consider hiring professional property management services to handle tenant screening, rent collection, property maintenance, and other administrative tasks. This can help ensure efficient operations and maximize returns.

5. Long-Term Investment Strategy: Focus on building a portfolio of residential properties for long-term wealth accumulation. By holding properties for an extended period, you can benefit from rental income, property appreciation, and potential tax advantages.

6. Risk Management: Diversify your residential property portfolio across different locations and property types to mitigate risk. Additionally, maintain adequate insurance coverage and set aside contingency funds for unexpected expenses.

7. Market Timing: Consider market cycles and economic conditions when making investment decisions. Timing the market can help you capitalize on opportunities during favorable conditions.

8. Network and Partnerships: Build a network of professionals, including real estate agents, lenders, contractors, and fellow investors. Collaborating with knowledgeable partners can provide valuable insights and enhance your investment strategies.

Implementing these strategies can help increase the profitability of residential real estate investments. However, it's important to adapt and refine your approach based on market conditions and individual property characteristics. Conducting thorough due diligence, staying informed about market trends, and seeking professional advice when needed are key to successful residential investment strategies.

Buy and Hold Strategy: Long-Term Rental Income and Property Appreciation

The buy and hold strategy is a popular approach in residential real estate investing, focusing on long-term rental income and property appreciation. Here's how this strategy works:

1. Property Acquisition: Identify properties with good rental potential and long-term value appreciation. Conduct thorough research, including market analysis, property condition assessment, and financial feasibility.

2. Cash Flow Generation: Purchase properties that generate positive cash flow from rental income after accounting for expenses like mortgage payments, taxes, insurance, and maintenance costs.

3. Tenant Selection and Management: Implement effective tenant screening processes to secure reliable and responsible tenants. Maintain regular communication and ensure proper property maintenance to minimize vacancy periods and protect your investment.

4. Equity Building: Over time, rental income and property appreciation contribute to building equity. Equity accumulation allows you to leverage your investments for future acquisitions or financing opportunities.

5. Tax Advantages: Take advantage of tax benefits such as deductible expenses (e.g., mortgage interest, property taxes) and depreciation deductions, which can help optimize your cash flow.

6. Long-Term Wealth Accumulation: By holding properties for an extended period, you can benefit from rental income, potential property appreciation, and wealth accumulation. This strategy aligns with a patient and disciplined investment approach.

7. Portfolio Diversification: As you grow your real estate portfolio, consider diversifying across different property types, locations, and rental markets. This helps spread risk and capture potential growth in various markets.

While the buy and hold strategy offers potential long-term rewards, it requires careful property selection, diligent management, and a focus on market trends. It is essential to consider your investment goals, financial capabilities, and risk tolerance before adopting this strategy. Patience, adaptability, and a long-term perspective are key to success when implementing the buy and hold strategy in residential real estate investing.

House Flipping: Buying, Renovating, and Selling Properties for Quick Profits

House flipping is a real estate investment strategy focused on purchasing properties, renovating them, and selling them for a profit within a relatively short period. Here's an overview of the house flipping process:

1. Property Identification: Identify undervalued properties with potential for improvement. Look for distressed properties, foreclosures, or properties in need of repairs or upgrades.

2. Financial Analysis: Conduct a thorough financial analysis, considering the purchase price, renovation costs, holding costs, and potential selling price. Ensure that the expected profit margin justifies the investment.

3. Renovation Planning: Develop a detailed renovation plan, considering cosmetic upgrades, structural repairs, and enhancements that will add value to the property. Set a budget and timeline for the renovations.

4. Renovation Execution: Oversee the renovation process, hiring contractors or completing the renovations yourself if you have the necessary skills. Stay within budget and timeline to maximize profitability.

5. Marketing and Sale: Once the renovations are complete, market the property effectively to attract potential buyers. Utilize various marketing channels, such as online listings, open houses, and real estate agents, to generate interest.

6. Profit Generation: Sell the property at a higher price than the total investment, including the purchase price and renovation costs. The difference between the selling price and total investment represents the profit.

7. Risk Management: House flipping involves risks such as unexpected renovation costs, market fluctuations, and longer-than-anticipated holding periods. Mitigate risks through thorough due diligence, realistic budgeting, and contingency planning.

House flipping can offer significant profits in a relatively short timeframe. However, it requires careful property selection, renovation expertise, and market knowledge. It's crucial to accurately assess costs, accurately estimate selling prices, and stay within budget to achieve desired profitability. Successful house flipping relies on efficient project management, effective marketing, and a keen eye for identifying opportunities in the real estate market.

Rent-to-Own and Lease Options: Alternative Strategies for Income Generation

Rent-to-own and lease options are alternative strategies in real estate that offer income generation opportunities. Here's how these strategies work:

1. Rent-to-Own: In a rent-to-own arrangement, a tenant has the option to purchase the property at a predetermined price within a specified timeframe. Part of the rent payments may be credited toward the purchase price, serving as a form of down payment accumulation.

2. Lease Options: Lease options grant the tenant the right, but not the obligation, to buy the property at a predetermined price during or at the end of the lease term. This provides flexibility for tenants who may not be ready to commit to a purchase immediately.

3. Income Generation: Rent payments from tenants in rent-to-own and lease option agreements serve as a source of regular income for property owners. These arrangements often command higher rental rates, as tenants pay for the opportunity to exercise the purchase option.

4. Tenant Qualification: It's crucial to screen potential tenants thoroughly to ensure they have the financial capacity and commitment to fulfill

the purchase option. Consider factors such as credit history, income stability, and the willingness to maintain the property.

5. Legal Considerations: Engage legal professionals to draft comprehensive rent-to-own or lease option agreements that clearly outline the rights and obligations of both parties, including the purchase terms and conditions.

6. Property Maintenance: As the property owner, it's essential to maintain the property's condition and address any necessary repairs or maintenance during the rental period. This helps preserve the property's value and attractiveness to potential buyers.

7. Risk Management: Assess the risks associated with rent-to-own and lease options, such as tenant default or changes in market conditions. Mitigate risks by setting clear contractual terms, conducting regular property inspections, and staying informed about the local real estate market.

Rent-to-own and lease options provide alternative income generation strategies for property owners. These arrangements offer potential long-term benefits, including higher rental income, potential property appreciation, and the possibility of a successful sale. However, it's important to understand the legal and financial implications of these strategies and seek professional advice when necessary.

Section 2: Commercial Real Estate Investments

In this section, we will delve into the realm of commercial real estate investments. Commercial properties encompass a wide range of assets, including office buildings, retail spaces, industrial properties, and more. Investing in commercial real estate offers unique opportunities and challenges compared to residential properties. We will explore various aspects of commercial real estate investments, including market dynamics, property types, financing options, and strategies for success. Whether you are a seasoned investor or new to the world of commercial real estate, this section will provide valuable insights to help you navigate the complexities of this investment avenue.

2.1 Exploring Commercial Real Estate:

Introduction to commercial real estate and its different asset classes

Commercial real estate encompasses a wide range of properties used for business purposes, such as office buildings, retail spaces, industrial facilities, and multifamily residential complexes. Unlike residential real estate, commercial properties are primarily focused on generating income through rent or lease payments from businesses.

Understanding the different asset classes within commercial real estate is essential for investors seeking to diversify their portfolios and capitalize on specific market opportunities. Here are some of the key asset classes in commercial real estate:

1. Office Buildings: These properties cater to businesses needing office space, ranging from small startups to large corporate headquarters. Office buildings can be classified into Class A (high-quality, well-located, and modern), Class B (older buildings with some updates), or Class C (older buildings in less desirable locations).

2. Retail Properties: This asset class includes shopping centers, malls, standalone retail buildings, and mixed-use developments. Retail properties serve as spaces for retailers, restaurants, and other consumer-oriented businesses. Retail properties can be classified based on location, size, tenant mix, and market demand.

3. Industrial Properties: Industrial real estate includes warehouses, distribution centers, manufacturing facilities, and logistics properties. These properties are vital for the storage, production, and movement of goods. Industrial properties can vary in size, configuration, and

specialization, catering to different industry sectors.

4. Multifamily Residential: Multifamily properties comprise apartment buildings, condominiums, and residential complexes. These properties generate income through rental payments from tenants. Multifamily residential properties can offer steady cash flow and potential appreciation, making them attractive investment options.

5. Hospitality: This asset class includes hotels, resorts, and other lodging properties. Hospitality properties cater to travelers and tourists, generating revenue through room bookings, dining services, and event hosting.

6. Mixed-Use Developments: These properties combine multiple asset classes, such as retail, office, residential, and entertainment spaces within a single development. Mixed-use projects aim to create vibrant, self-contained communities that offer convenience and a variety of amenities.

Understanding the nuances of each asset class is crucial for investors to make informed decisions and align their investment goals with market opportunities. By diversifying across different commercial real estate asset classes, investors can mitigate risk and potentially achieve attractive returns.

Office buildings, retail spaces, industrial properties, and more

Commercial real estate offers a diverse array of investment opportunities across various asset classes. From office buildings and retail spaces to industrial properties and more, each asset class has its unique characteristics and potential for returns. Let's take a closer look at these commercial real estate asset classes:

1. Office Buildings: These properties serve as workplaces for businesses, ranging from small startups to multinational corporations. Office buildings can be located in central business districts or suburban areas, offering a wide range of lease options and amenities.

2. Retail Spaces: Retail properties include shopping centers, malls, strip malls, and standalone retail buildings. These spaces are leased to retailers and service providers, catering to the needs of consumers and generating rental income.

3. Industrial Properties: Industrial real estate comprises warehouses, distribution centers, manufacturing facilities, and logistics properties. These properties support various industries by providing storage, production, and distribution spaces.

4. Multifamily Residential: Multifamily properties consist of apartment buildings and residential complexes where tenants rent living spaces. These properties can range from small apartment buildings to high-rise condominiums, offering a steady income stream.

5. Hospitality: The hospitality sector encompasses hotels, resorts, and other lodging properties. These assets cater to travelers and tourists, providing accommodations, dining options, and event spaces.

6. Mixed-Use Developments: Mixed-use properties combine multiple asset classes, such as residential, retail, office, and entertainment spaces within a single development. These developments aim to create vibrant, self-contained communities that offer convenience and a diverse range of amenities.

By diversifying investments across these commercial real estate asset classes, investors can tap into various sectors of the economy, manage risk, and potentially achieve attractive returns. Each asset class presents unique challenges and opportunities, requiring careful analysis and market understanding for successful investment decisions.

Key factors influencing the commercial real estate market

The commercial real estate market is influenced by various factors that shape its dynamics and investment potential. Understanding these key factors is crucial for investors seeking to navigate this market effectively. Here are some of the primary factors that influence the commercial real estate market:

1. Economic Conditions: The overall health of the economy, including factors such as GDP growth, employment rates, and consumer spending, directly impacts the demand for commercial real estate. Economic downturns can lead to decreased demand and lower occupancy rates, while robust economic growth can drive increased demand for commercial properties.

2. Supply and Demand Dynamics: The balance between supply and demand plays a significant role in determining property values and rental rates. A scarcity of available properties in high-demand areas can drive up prices, while an oversupply of properties can lead to lower occupancy rates and decreased rental income.

3. Location: Location is a critical factor in commercial real estate. Properties in prime locations with high visibility, accessibility, and proximity to amenities tend to attract higher

demand and command premium rents. The desirability of a location can be influenced by factors such as population growth, demographics, infrastructure development, and proximity to business hubs.

4. Interest Rates: Interest rates have a direct impact on borrowing costs, which affects financing options for commercial real estate investments. Lower interest rates can make borrowing more affordable, stimulating investment activity in the market. Conversely, higher interest rates can increase borrowing costs and potentially dampen demand.

5. Market Sentiment and Investor Confidence: Market sentiment and investor confidence play a significant role in shaping the commercial real estate market. Positive sentiment and high investor confidence can drive increased investment activity and demand for commercial properties. Conversely, negative sentiment or uncertainty can lead to cautious investor behavior and slower market activity.

6. Regulatory and Legal Factors: Regulatory and legal factors, such as zoning regulations, building codes, tax policies, and lease laws, can significantly impact the commercial real estate market. Changes in regulations or tax laws can influence investment strategies and the overall profitability of commercial real estate ventures.

By keeping a close eye on these key factors and their evolving trends, investors can gain valuable insights into the commercial real estate market and make informed investment decisions. Understanding the interplay of these factors allows investors to identify opportunities, mitigate risks, and maximize their potential returns.

2.2 Financing Commercial Investments

In this section, we will delve into the realm of financing commercial real estate investments. Commercial properties often require substantial capital investments, and understanding the financing options available is crucial for investors. We will explore various financing avenues, including traditional bank loans, commercial mortgages, private equity, and crowdfunding platforms. Additionally, we will discuss the importance of creditworthiness, loan-to-value ratios, and debt service coverage ratios in securing financing for commercial investments. By gaining insights into the financing landscape, investors can make informed decisions to structure their commercial real estate investments and optimize their returns.

Financing Options for Commercial Real Estate Investments

Financing commercial real estate investments requires careful consideration of the available options. Here are some common financing avenues for commercial properties:

1. Traditional Bank Loans: Commercial mortgages from banks and financial institutions are a popular choice. These loans typically have fixed or variable interest rates and require a down payment and collateral. The terms and eligibility criteria vary based on factors such as creditworthiness, property type, and loan amount.

2. Commercial Mortgage-Backed Securities (CMBS): CMBS loans are a type of securitized financing where loans are pooled together and sold as securities to investors. These loans are often used for large-scale commercial properties and can offer competitive rates and flexible terms.

3. Private Equity: Investors can seek private equity funding, where they partner with private investors or firms. This option allows for more flexibility in terms of loan structure and repayment.

4. Crowdfunding Platforms: Crowdfunding has emerged as an alternative financing option for commercial real estate. Through online platforms, investors can pool their resources to fund

commercial projects in exchange for equity or debt-based returns.

5. Seller Financing: In some cases, the property owner may provide financing to the buyer, acting as the lender. This option can be negotiated directly between the parties and may offer more flexible terms.

6. Small Business Administration (SBA) Loans: The SBA offers loan programs specifically designed to support small businesses acquiring or refinancing commercial real estate. These loans typically have favorable terms and lower down payment requirements.

It's essential for investors to carefully evaluate the terms, interest rates, repayment schedules, and eligibility criteria of each financing option. Consulting with financial advisors and mortgage professionals can help navigate the complexities of commercial real estate financing and choose the most suitable option for individual investment goals and circumstances.

Commercial Mortgages, Equity Partnerships, and Syndication: Financing Options for Commercial Real Estate Investments

When it comes to financing commercial real estate investments, there are several options available.

Let's explore three common financing strategies: commercial mortgages, equity partnerships, and syndication.

1. Commercial Mortgages: This traditional financing option involves securing a loan from a bank or financial institution specifically tailored for commercial properties. The borrower provides collateral, such as the property itself, and makes regular mortgage payments over a set period. Commercial mortgages offer competitive interest rates and terms, with the property serving as security for the loan.

2. Equity Partnerships: In an equity partnership, multiple parties pool their resources to invest in a commercial property. Each partner contributes capital, and their ownership stake reflects their investment. This option allows for shared financial responsibility, risk, and potential returns. Equity partnerships often involve creating a legal entity, such as a limited partnership or limited liability company, to govern the partnership.

3. Syndication: Syndication involves raising capital from multiple investors to fund a commercial real estate project. A syndicator, typically an experienced real estate professional or firm, identifies investment opportunities and structures the deal. Investors can participate in the project with varying levels of investment and

expected returns. Syndication offers individual investors the opportunity to access larger-scale projects and diversify their investment portfolios.

Each financing option has its own advantages and considerations. Commercial mortgages provide traditional borrowing options, equity partnerships allow for shared ownership, and syndication offers access to larger-scale projects. Investors should carefully evaluate the terms, risks, and potential returns associated with each option to determine the most suitable approach for their commercial real estate investments.

Assessing the Financial Feasibility of Commercial Investments

Before diving into commercial real estate investments, it's crucial to assess the financial feasibility of the opportunities at hand. Here are some key factors to consider:

1. Market Analysis: Conduct a thorough market analysis to understand the demand and supply dynamics of the specific commercial property type and location. Evaluate factors such as vacancy rates, rental rates, and market trends to gauge the potential for income generation.

2. Cash Flow Projections: Prepare detailed cash flow projections, considering both rental income

and expenses such as property taxes, maintenance costs, insurance, and property management fees. Ensure that the projected cash flow is sufficient to cover expenses and generate a positive net operating income.

3. Return on Investment (ROI): Calculate the potential ROI by factoring in the purchase price, financing costs, rental income, and projected property appreciation over the holding period. Compare the ROI with industry benchmarks and consider the risk associated with the investment.

4. Financing Considerations: Evaluate financing options, including interest rates, loan terms, and down payment requirements. Assess the impact of financing costs on the cash flow and overall profitability of the investment.

5. Risk Assessment: Identify and analyze potential risks associated with the investment, such as market fluctuations, tenant turnover, lease renewals, and regulatory changes. Develop risk mitigation strategies to protect your investment.

6. Exit Strategy: Consider the potential exit options for the investment, such as selling the property, refinancing, or converting it into another use. Assess the potential returns and liquidity of each exit strategy.

By conducting a comprehensive financial feasibility analysis, you can make informed investment decisions and increase the likelihood of success in your commercial real estate ventures. Seek advice from real estate professionals, financial advisors, and conduct due diligence to ensure a thorough evaluation of the investment's financial viability.

2.3 Strategies for Successful Commercial Investments

In this section, we will explore strategies for achieving success in commercial real estate investments. Commercial properties offer unique opportunities and require careful planning and execution. Let's discuss some key strategies to consider:

1. Thorough Due Diligence: Conduct comprehensive due diligence to evaluate the property's financials, lease agreements, tenant history, and market conditions. This includes analyzing income and expense statements, reviewing lease terms, and assessing the property's condition. Thorough due diligence helps identify potential risks and opportunities.

2. Location Analysis: Select commercial properties in prime locations with high growth potential and demand. Consider factors such as proximity to

transportation hubs, demographics, local economic indicators, and future development plans. A strategic location can significantly impact the property's value and potential for long-term success.

3. Tenant Quality and Stability: Focus on attracting high-quality tenants with strong financial stability and track records. Evaluate tenant creditworthiness, lease terms, and industry prospects. A diverse tenant mix and long-term lease agreements contribute to stable cash flow and minimize vacancy risks.

4. Property Management: Implement effective property management strategies to maximize returns. This includes regular property maintenance, tenant relationship management, lease renewals, and proactive vacancy management. Well-managed properties attract and retain quality tenants and enhance overall investment performance.

5. Value-Add Opportunities: Look for value-add opportunities where property improvements or repositioning can increase its value and income potential. Renovations, lease renegotiations, or adding amenities can attract higher-paying tenants and improve cash flow.

6. Risk Mitigation: Develop risk mitigation strategies to protect your investment. This

includes diversifying your portfolio, maintaining adequate insurance coverage, and having contingency plans for unexpected events.

7. Long-Term Vision: Adopt a long-term investment approach and focus on building sustainable wealth through commercial real estate. While short-term fluctuations may occur, commercial properties often appreciate over time, providing consistent income and potential for capital appreciation.

By implementing these strategies and adapting them to your specific investment goals and circumstances, you can enhance the likelihood of success in commercial real estate investments.

Commercial Leasing: Long-Term Tenants and Stable Income Streams

One of the key strategies for successful commercial real estate investments is securing long-term tenants and establishing stable income streams through commercial leasing. Here's why it's important and how to achieve it:

1. Stability and Predictability: Long-term leases provide stability by ensuring a consistent rental income stream over an extended period. This stability allows investors to plan their cash flow and financial projections with greater certainty.

2. Tenant Selection: Carefully select tenants with strong financial stability, reputable track records, and a commitment to long-term occupancy. Thoroughly vet potential tenants, including analyzing their financial statements, creditworthiness, and business plans.

3. Negotiating Favorable Lease Terms: Structure leases with favorable terms that benefit both the landlord and the tenant. Consider factors such as lease duration, rent escalations, maintenance responsibilities, and lease renewal options. Striking a balance between fair terms and attractive incentives can help attract and retain high-quality, long-term tenants.

4. Building Tenant Relationships: Foster positive relationships with tenants by maintaining open lines of communication, addressing their needs, and providing excellent property management services. Happy tenants are more likely to renew their leases and maintain a long-term occupancy, reducing turnover and associated costs.

5. Property Maintenance and Upgrades: Ensure proper property maintenance and periodic upgrades to meet tenant expectations and attract long-term occupants. Well-maintained properties create a positive image, enhance tenant satisfaction, and contribute to tenant retention.

6. Market Research and Analysis: Stay informed about market trends, rental rates, and tenant demands in the commercial real estate market. Understanding the market dynamics allows you to adjust your leasing strategies accordingly and attract suitable long-term tenants.

7. Lease Renewal Planning: Proactively engage with tenants as lease expiration approaches to discuss renewal options. Offer incentives, such as rent concessions or tenant improvements, to encourage lease extensions. Early renewal discussions help maintain occupancy levels and minimize periods of vacancy.

By focusing on securing long-term tenants and establishing stable income streams through commercial leasing, investors can enjoy consistent cash flow and mitigate risks associated with tenant turnover. A well-managed leasing strategy contributes to the long-term success and profitability of commercial real estate investments.

Development and Redevelopment Projects: Creating Value Through Construction and Revitalization

Development and redevelopment projects are key strategies for creating value in the world of real estate. By engaging in construction and revitalization efforts, investors can unlock the full potential of properties and generate substantial returns. Here's why these projects are important and how they contribute to value creation:

1. Property Transformation: Development projects involve constructing new buildings or expanding existing ones, while redevelopment projects focus on revitalizing underutilized or outdated properties. Through these projects, investors can transform properties into modern, functional, and attractive spaces that meet the evolving needs of tenants and buyers.

2. Increased Market Demand: Well-executed development and redevelopment projects can attract a larger pool of potential tenants or buyers, driving up market demand. This increased demand can result in higher rental or selling prices, maximizing the return on investment.

3. Improved Property Performance: Construction and revitalization efforts can enhance a property's performance by introducing modern amenities, energy-efficient features, and state-of-the-art infrastructure. These upgrades not only improve the overall tenant or buyer experience but also increase the property's desirability and competitiveness in the market.

4. Neighborhood Enhancement: Development and redevelopment projects can have a positive impact

on the surrounding neighborhood or community. By revitalizing blighted areas or bringing new life to vacant lots, these projects contribute to the overall economic growth and attractiveness of the location.

5. Job Creation and Economic Stimulus: Construction projects create employment opportunities and stimulate the local economy. They generate jobs for architects, contractors, engineers, and various skilled trades, supporting economic growth and providing a ripple effect of economic benefits.

6. Adaptive Reuse and Sustainability: Redevelopment projects often involve repurposing existing structures, promoting sustainability and preserving the historical or cultural value of the property. Adaptive reuse not only minimizes waste but also adds unique character to the development, attracting environmentally conscious tenants or buyers.

7. Profit Potential: Successful development and redevelopment projects can yield substantial profits. By adding value through construction, modernization, and strategic improvements, investors can capitalize on the increased market demand and command higher rental income or sale prices.

However, it's important to note that development and redevelopment projects come with their own set of challenges, such as regulatory requirements, construction risks, and market uncertainties. Thorough feasibility studies, careful planning, and diligent project management are crucial to mitigate these risks and ensure the success of these ventures.

Overall, development and redevelopment projects offer exciting opportunities to create value, revitalize communities, and generate attractive returns on real estate investments.

Niche Commercial Sectors: Exploring Opportunities in Healthcare, Hospitality, and More

When it comes to commercial real estate investments, exploring niche sectors can unlock unique opportunities for investors. These specialized sectors, such as healthcare and hospitality, offer distinct advantages and the potential for high returns. Here's a closer look at some niche commercial sectors worth considering:

1. Healthcare: The healthcare sector encompasses medical offices, clinics, hospitals, and senior living facilities. With an aging population and increasing demand for healthcare services, investing in

healthcare properties can provide stable income streams and long-term growth potential.

2. Hospitality: The hospitality sector includes hotels, resorts, vacation rentals, and event venues. It thrives on tourism, business travel, and leisure activities. Investing in hospitality properties allows investors to capitalize on the growing hospitality industry and potentially benefit from seasonal demand and attractive rental yields.

3. Data Centers: As the digital age progresses, the demand for data centers continues to rise. Data centers are critical infrastructure for storing and processing vast amounts of digital information. Investing in data centers can offer stable cash flow and the potential for long-term appreciation as the demand for data storage and cloud computing expands.

4. Self-Storage: Self-storage facilities provide individuals and businesses with space to store their belongings. The self-storage sector has shown resilience even during economic downturns and can provide consistent rental income. As urbanization and downsizing trends continue, investing in self-storage properties can be a lucrative opportunity.

5. Mixed-Use Developments: Mixed-use developments combine residential, commercial, and retail spaces within a single project. These

developments create vibrant communities and cater to diverse needs, attracting tenants, buyers, and visitors. Investing in mixed-use developments can offer a range of income streams and potential for capital appreciation.

6. Student Housing: With a growing student population, investing in student housing can provide a stable rental market. Proximity to educational institutions and amenities is crucial for this sector's success. Student housing properties can offer steady cash flow and the potential for high occupancy rates.

7. Industrial and Logistics: The rise of e-commerce has fueled the demand for industrial and logistics properties, including warehouses, distribution centers, and fulfillment centers. Investing in this sector can capitalize on the growth of online retail and logistics operations, offering stable rental income and potential capital appreciation.

While these niche sectors present exciting opportunities, it's important to conduct thorough market research, assess the local demand and supply dynamics, and understand the specific challenges associated with each sector. Partnering with industry experts and professionals can provide valuable insights and guidance for successful investments in niche commercial sectors.

By exploring opportunities in niche commercial sectors such as healthcare, hospitality, data centers, self-storage, mixed-use developments, student housing, and industrial logistics, investors can diversify their portfolios and tap into sectors with unique growth potential and favorable market dynamics.

Section 3: Real Estate Investment Trusts (REITs)

Real Estate Investment Trusts (REITs) offer investors a convenient and accessible way to participate in the real estate market. In this section, we will explore the ins and outs of REITs and their role in real estate investing. Here are the key topics covered:

1. Introduction to REITs: Learn about the concept and structure of REITs, which are companies that own, operate, or finance income-generating real estate. Discover how REITs provide investors with an opportunity to invest in a diversified portfolio of properties across different sectors.

2. Types of REITs: Explore the various types of REITs, including equity REITs, mortgage REITs, and hybrid REITs. Understand the differences in their investment strategies, income sources, and risk profiles.

3. Benefits of Investing in REITs: Discover the advantages of including REITs in your investment portfolio, such as potential high dividends, liquidity, professional management, and the ability to invest in real estate without directly owning properties.

4. Assessing REIT Performance: Learn how to evaluate the performance of REITs by analyzing key metrics such as funds from operations (FFO), net operating income (NOI), occupancy rates, and dividend yield. Understand the importance of conducting thorough due diligence before investing in REITs.

5. Tax Considerations: Explore the tax implications of investing in REITs, including the requirement for REITs to distribute a significant portion of their taxable income to shareholders as dividends, which can result in favorable tax treatment for investors.

6. REIT Investment Strategies: Discover different strategies for investing in REITs, such as investing in specific property sectors, geographic regions, or focusing on growth-oriented or income-oriented REITs based on your investment objectives.

7. Risks and Challenges: Understand the potential risks associated with investing in REITs, including interest rate risk, market volatility, regulatory changes, and specific risks related to the property sectors in which the REIT operates.

8. Real Estate Mutual Funds and ETFs: Explore alternative investment vehicles, such as real estate mutual funds and exchange-traded funds (ETFs), which provide exposure to a diversified portfolio of REITs.

By delving into the world of REITs, investors can gain access to the benefits of real estate investing while enjoying liquidity, professional management, and potential income generation. However, it's important to carefully consider the risks, perform thorough research, and consult with financial professionals before making investment decisions related to REITs.

3.1 Understanding REITs

Before diving into investing in Real Estate Investment Trusts (REITs), it's crucial to gain a comprehensive understanding of their structure and functioning. In this section, we will explore the fundamental aspects of REITs, including:

1. Definition and Purpose: Learn what exactly a REIT is and how it operates within the real estate market. Discover the primary objective of REITs, which is to generate income through property investments.

2. Legal Requirements: Understand the legal framework that governs REITs, including the necessary qualifications and regulations they must adhere to in order to qualify for special tax treatment.

3. Property Ownership and Management: Explore how REITs acquire and manage properties. Learn about the various types of real estate assets that can be held by REITs, such as commercial properties, residential complexes, and even infrastructure projects.

4. Income Generation: Gain insights into how REITs generate income, primarily through rental revenues from their properties. Understand how the income is distributed to shareholders in the form of dividends.

5. Shareholder Benefits: Discover the advantages of investing in REITs, such as access to a diverse portfolio of properties, professional management, and the potential for regular dividend income.

6. Different REIT Structures: Learn about the various types of REIT structures, including equity REITs, mortgage REITs, and hybrid REITs. Understand their distinct characteristics and investment strategies.

7. Market Performance: Explore historical performance trends of REITs and understand how they have performed in different market conditions. Gain insights into the factors that influence the valuation and growth potential of REITs.

By grasping the fundamental aspects of REITs, investors can make informed decisions and leverage the benefits of these investment vehicles. However, it's essential to continue exploring the intricacies of REITs, including the specific risks, tax considerations, and market dynamics associated with investing in this asset class.

Introduction to Real Estate Investment Trusts and Their Structure

Real Estate Investment Trusts (REITs) are investment vehicles that allow individuals to invest in income-generating real estate properties without directly owning or managing them. In this section, we will provide an introduction to REITs and delve into their structure. Here are the key points covered:

1. Definition and Purpose: Understand what REITs are and how they function as companies that own, operate, or finance income-producing real estate assets. Discover how REITs enable investors to access the real estate market and benefit from rental income and property appreciation.

2. Legal Structure: Explore the legal requirements and structure of REITs, including the need to meet specific criteria to qualify for favorable tax treatment. Learn about the regulations and

guidelines that govern the formation and operation of REITs.

3. Shareholder Ownership: Discover how REITs are structured as publicly traded companies, with shares of ownership held by individual investors. Understand how shareholders participate in the potential returns generated by the underlying real estate investments.

4. Property Portfolio: Gain insights into the types of real estate assets that REITs typically invest in, such as office buildings, shopping centers, apartment complexes, industrial properties, and more. Learn how REITs diversify their property portfolios to mitigate risk.

5. Income Distribution: Learn about the unique requirement for REITs to distribute a significant portion of their taxable income to shareholders in the form of dividends. Understand how this distribution allows REIT investors to benefit from regular income streams.

6. Professional Management: Explore how REITs are managed by experienced professionals who oversee property acquisitions, leasing, maintenance, and other operational aspects. Understand the advantages of having skilled management teams in place.

By understanding the basics of REITs and their structure, investors can evaluate the potential benefits and risks associated with investing in this asset class. It is important to conduct thorough research, assess individual REITs based on their property holdings and financial performance, and consider personal investment goals and risk tolerance before making investment decisions in the REIT market.

Benefits of Investing in REITs: Liquidity, Diversification, and Professional Management
Investing in Real Estate Investment Trusts (REITs) offers several advantages that make them an attractive option for investors seeking exposure to the real estate market. In this section, we will explore the benefits of investing in REITs, including:

1. Liquidity: REITs are publicly traded on stock exchanges, providing investors with the ability to buy and sell shares easily. This liquidity allows investors to enter or exit their positions quickly, providing flexibility and access to their investment capital.

2. Diversification: REITs offer diversification benefits by pooling investors' funds to invest in a wide range of real estate properties across different sectors and geographies. This diversification helps spread risk and reduces

exposure to any single property or market segment.

3. Professional Management: REITs are managed by experienced professionals who have the expertise and knowledge to identify, acquire, and manage real estate properties effectively. Investors benefit from the professional management teams' ability to handle property operations, tenant management, and strategic decision-making.

4. Income Generation: REITs are required to distribute a significant portion of their taxable income to shareholders in the form of dividends. This regular income stream provides investors with the potential for consistent cash flow, making REITs appealing for those seeking regular income in their investment portfolio.

5. Potential for Capital Appreciation: In addition to income generation, REITs have the potential for capital appreciation. As the underlying real estate properties appreciate in value over time, the value of the REIT shares may also increase, allowing investors to benefit from potential capital gains.

6. Accessibility: REITs provide individual investors with access to the real estate market, which may otherwise require substantial capital and expertise to invest directly in properties. REITs offer a more accessible and convenient way

for investors to participate in the potential returns of real estate investments.

It's important to note that investing in REITs carries risks, such as market fluctuations, interest rate changes, and specific risks related to the real estate sector. Investors should conduct thorough research, assess the performance and financial health of individual REITs, and consider their own investment goals and risk tolerance before making investment decisions in this asset class.

Different Types of REITs and Their Investment Strategies

Real Estate Investment Trusts (REITs) encompass various types, each focusing on specific segments of the real estate market. In this section, we will explore the different types of REITs and their investment strategies. Here are some key categories:

1. Equity REITs: These REITs invest in and own income-generating properties such as office buildings, shopping centers, residential complexes, and industrial facilities. Their primary strategy is to generate rental income and capital appreciation through property ownership and management.

2. Mortgage REITs: Instead of owning properties, these REITs provide financing for real estate by

investing in mortgages and other real estate-related loans. They earn income through interest payments and loan origination fees.

3. Hybrid REITs: These REITs combine elements of both equity and mortgage REITs. They may own properties while also investing in real estate debt instruments. This hybrid approach aims to benefit from a diversified income stream.

4. Retail REITs: Specializing in retail properties such as shopping malls, strip centers, and freestanding retail buildings, these REITs focus on leasing to retail tenants and generating rental income.

5. Residential REITs: These REITs primarily invest in residential properties such as apartment buildings, single-family homes, and multifamily complexes. They generate income from rental payments.

6. Office REITs: These REITs specialize in office buildings and generate rental income from leasing office spaces to businesses and organizations.

7. Industrial REITs: Focusing on industrial properties such as warehouses, distribution centers, and manufacturing facilities, these REITs aim to generate income from leasing to industrial tenants.

8. Healthcare REITs: These REITs invest in healthcare-related properties, such as hospitals, medical office buildings, senior living facilities, and specialized care centers. They generate income from leasing to healthcare providers.

9. Hotel and Resort REITs: These REITs own and operate hotels, resorts, and other hospitality properties. They generate income from guest stays and related services.

Each type of REIT has its own investment strategy and focuses on specific segments of the real estate market. It's important for investors to consider their investment goals, risk tolerance, and market conditions when selecting REITs for their portfolio. Conducting thorough research and understanding the specific investment strategies of different REITs can help investors make informed decisions and build a diversified real estate investment portfolio.

3.2 Evaluating and Investing in REITs

Investing in Real Estate Investment Trusts (REITs) requires careful evaluation to make informed investment decisions. In this section, we will explore the key factors to consider when evaluating and investing in REITs. Here are some important points to keep in mind:

1. Financial Performance: Assess the REIT's financial health by analyzing its historical and current financial performance, including revenue growth, net operating income, funds from operations (FFO), and dividend history. Evaluate key financial ratios and metrics to gauge the REIT's profitability, liquidity, and leverage.

2. Property Portfolio: Examine the quality, diversity, and geographic spread of the REIT's property portfolio. Consider factors such as property types, occupancy rates, lease terms, and tenant profiles. A well-diversified portfolio across different property sectors and locations can mitigate risks.

3. Management Team: Evaluate the REIT's management team's experience, expertise, and track record in the real estate industry. Consider their ability to execute the REIT's investment strategy, asset management, and operational efficiency.

4. Dividend Policy: Understand the REIT's dividend policy, including the distribution rate, frequency, and consistency of dividend payments. Evaluate the REIT's ability to generate sustainable rental income to support dividend payments.

5. Market Analysis: Assess the market conditions and trends affecting the REIT's property sectors.

Consider factors such as supply and demand dynamics, rental rates, vacancy rates, and economic indicators that can impact the REIT's performance.

6. Regulatory Environment: Understand the regulatory framework governing REITs in the relevant jurisdiction. Evaluate any specific regulations, tax implications, and compliance requirements that may affect the REIT's operations and profitability.

7. Risk Factors: Identify and assess the risks associated with investing in the specific type of REIT, such as market risks, interest rate risks, tenant concentration risks, and operational risks. Consider how the REIT's risk profile aligns with your risk tolerance and investment objectives.

8. Valuation: Determine whether the REIT is trading at a fair valuation compared to its underlying assets, earnings, and industry peers. Evaluate metrics such as price-to-FFO ratio and price-to-net asset value to assess the REIT's valuation relative to its earnings and asset value.

By thoroughly evaluating these factors, investors can make more informed decisions when investing in REITs. It's important to conduct due diligence, review financial statements and disclosures, and consult with financial professionals to gain a comprehensive understanding of the REIT's potential risks and rewards.

Analyzing REIT Performance: Key Metrics and Indicators

When analyzing the performance of Real Estate Investment Trusts (REITs), there are several key metrics and indicators that can provide valuable insights. Here are some important ones to consider:

1. Funds From Operations (FFO): FFO is a widely used metric for evaluating REITs. It measures the cash flow generated by the REIT's operating activities, excluding gains or losses from property sales and non-operating items. FFO provides an indication of the REIT's ability to generate sustainable income from its properties.

2. Net Operating Income (NOI): NOI represents the REIT's total revenue from its properties, minus operating expenses, but before deducting interest and income taxes. It reflects the profitability of the REIT's core operations and is an important measure of its property portfolio's performance.

3. Dividend Yield: Dividend yield is the annual dividend payment of the REIT divided by its share price, expressed as a percentage. It indicates the income generated by the REIT's dividends relative

to its share price and can be compared to other income-generating investments.

4. Occupancy Rate: The occupancy rate measures the percentage of leased space in the REIT's properties. A high occupancy rate indicates strong demand for the REIT's properties and a potential for stable rental income.

5. Weighted Average Lease Expiry (WALE): WALE represents the average remaining lease term across the REIT's property portfolio. It provides insight into the stability and predictability of the REIT's rental income stream.

6. Debt-to-Equity Ratio: This ratio compares the REIT's total debt to its shareholders' equity. It helps assess the REIT's leverage and its ability to manage its debt obligations.

7. Total Return: Total return reflects the combined performance of a REIT's stock price appreciation and dividend payments over a specific period. It provides a comprehensive measure of the REIT's overall performance for investors.

8. Price-to-FFO Ratio: This ratio compares the market price of the REIT's shares to its FFO per share. It is commonly used to evaluate the REIT's valuation relative to its earnings potential.

By analyzing these key metrics and indicators, investors can gain insights into the financial health, income generation capabilities, and overall performance of REITs. It's important to compare these metrics with industry benchmarks and historical trends to assess the REIT's relative performance and make informed investment decisions.

Researching and Selecting REITs for Investment

When it comes to investing in Real Estate Investment Trusts (REITs), thorough research and careful selection are essential. Here are some steps to consider when researching and selecting REITs for investment:

1. Define Investment Objectives: Determine your investment goals, risk tolerance, and desired income generation to guide your REIT selection process.

2. Conduct Market Research: Analyze the real estate market and identify sectors that align with your investment objectives. Consider factors such as supply and demand dynamics, rental rates, and growth potential.

3. Screen REITs: Utilize screening tools or platforms to narrow down your options based on

criteria such as property type, geographic location, size, and financial performance.

4. **Assess Financial Health:** Review the REIT's financial statements, including balance sheets, income statements, and cash flow statements. Evaluate metrics such as FFO, NOI, and debt levels to gauge the REIT's financial health.

5. **Analyze Dividend History:** Examine the REIT's dividend payment history, consistency, and growth. Look for sustainable dividend yields and a track record of reliable income distribution.

6. **Evaluate Property Portfolio:** Assess the quality, diversity, and geographic spread of the REIT's property holdings. Consider factors such as property types, occupancy rates, lease terms, and tenant profiles.

7. **Review Management Team:** Research the REIT's management team and their experience in the real estate industry. Evaluate their track record, expertise, and alignment with shareholder interests.

8. **Understand Risk Factors:** Identify and assess the risks associated with the REIT, such as market risks, interest rate risks, and tenant concentration risks. Evaluate how these risks align with your risk tolerance.

9. Compare Valuations: Compare the REIT's valuation metrics, such as price-to-FFO ratio, with industry peers to assess its relative value. Consider whether the REIT is trading at a reasonable price compared to its earnings potential.

10. Seek Professional Advice: Consult with financial professionals, such as financial advisors or real estate experts, to gain additional insights and guidance in the selection process.

Remember that investing in REITs carries risks, and it's important to diversify your portfolio and regularly review your investments. Conducting thorough research, understanding the fundamentals, and making informed decisions will increase your chances of selecting REITs that align with your investment objectives and deliver favorable returns.

Risks and Considerations Associated with REIT Investments

While Real Estate Investment Trusts (REITs) offer potential benefits, it's important to be aware of the risks and considerations involved. Here are some key factors to keep in mind:

1. Market Risk: REITs are subject to market fluctuations and economic conditions that can impact property values and rental incomes. Changes in interest rates, supply and demand dynamics, and overall market sentiment can affect the performance of REIT investments.

2. Interest Rate Risk: Rising interest rates can increase borrowing costs for REITs, impacting their profitability and valuations. REITs with significant debt exposure may be more vulnerable to interest rate fluctuations.

3. Property-Specific Risks: Factors such as property vacancies, tenant defaults, and property damage can affect rental income and property values. Location-specific risks, such as changes in local regulations or economic conditions, can also impact property performance.

4. Liquidity Risk: REITs may have limited liquidity compared to publicly traded stocks. Selling REIT shares may take time and could result in price volatility.

5. Dividend Variability: While REITs are required to distribute a significant portion of their income as dividends, the amount and consistency of dividend payments can vary. Economic downturns or financial challenges faced by specific properties can impact dividend payouts.

6. Tax Considerations: REIT distributions may have different tax implications compared to other investments. It's important to understand the tax implications at the individual level, including potential tax obligations and benefits.

7. Regulatory and Legal Risks: REITs are subject to regulatory requirements and may face compliance challenges or legal disputes that can impact their operations and financial performance.

8. Management Quality: The success of a REIT depends on the expertise and effectiveness of its management team. Poor decision-making, lack of experience, or conflicts of interest can negatively impact the performance of a REIT.

9. Industry and Sector Risks: Different property sectors within the real estate market can have unique risks. Factors such as changes in consumer behavior, technological advancements, or industry-specific challenges can impact the performance of REITs in those sectors.

10. Lack of Control: As a REIT investor, you have limited control over property management and decision-making. It's important to trust the REIT's management team and their ability to navigate challenges effectively.

Before investing in REITs, it's crucial to conduct thorough research, assess your risk tolerance, and seek professional advice. Diversifying your portfolio and staying informed about market trends and industry developments can help mitigate risks associated with REIT investments.

Recap of the Chapter's Key Points and Takeaways

In this chapter on Real Estate Investments, we covered various aspects of investing in both residential and commercial real estate, as well as Real Estate Investment Trusts (REITs). Here are the key points and takeaways:

1. Residential Real Estate:
• Understand the dynamics of the residential market and different property types.

• Consider factors such as location, property condition, and rental demand when evaluating residential investments.

• Explore financing options and assess the financial viability of residential investments.

• Strategies include buy and hold, house flipping, and rent-to-own.

2. Commercial Real Estate:
• Learn about different commercial property types and the factors influencing the commercial market.

• Explore financing options for commercial investments, such as commercial mortgages and equity partnerships.

• Assess the financial feasibility of commercial investments and consider leasing and development strategies.

3. Real Estate Investment Trusts (REITs):
• Understand the structure, benefits, and types of REITs.

• Evaluate REIT performance using key metrics and indicators.

• Research and select REITs based on financial health, property portfolio, and management team.

• Be aware of the risks associated with REIT investments, including market fluctuations and property-specific risks.

Overall, real estate investments offer opportunities for income generation, long-term appreciation, and portfolio diversification. It's important to conduct thorough research, assess risks, and make informed decisions based on your investment objectives and risk tolerance.

Emphasizing the Importance of Due Diligence
and Strategic Planning in Real Estate
Investments

One of the key takeaways from this chapter is the
critical importance of due diligence and strategic
planning when it comes to real estate investments.
Whether investing in residential properties,
commercial properties, or REITs, thorough
research and analysis are vital.

Due diligence involves conducting extensive
research on the market, property types, financing
options, and potential risks. This includes
analyzing market trends, property values, rental
demand, and regulatory factors.

Strategic planning entails setting clear investment
goals, developing a well-defined strategy, and
aligning it with your risk tolerance and financial
objectives. This involves selecting the right
investment approach, determining the
investment timeframe, and carefully considering
factors like property selection, financing
strategies, and exit plans.

By conducting due diligence and developing a
strategic plan, investors can minimize risks,
optimize returns, and make informed decisions in
their real estate investments. It's crucial to seek
professional advice, leverage market insights, and

stay updated on industry trends to make sound investment choices.

Encouragement to Unlock the Potential of Real Estate Investments for Wealth Creation

Real estate investments offer a unique opportunity to unlock the potential for wealth creation. Whether it's through residential properties, commercial ventures, or REITs, real estate has the power to generate substantial returns over time.

By understanding the dynamics of the market, conducting thorough research, and employing strategic investment approaches, individuals can tap into the wealth-building potential of real estate. The key lies in identifying promising opportunities, assessing risks, and making informed decisions.

Real estate investments can provide steady cash flow, long-term appreciation, tax advantages, and portfolio diversification. Moreover, they allow individuals to actively participate in the growth of tangible assets.

With diligence, patience, and the willingness to learn, investors can embark on a rewarding journey towards wealth creation through real estate investments. Start exploring the possibilities and unlock the potential of real estate to build lasting financial prosperity.

Idea: Purchase a Property for Rental Income or Capital Appreciation

One promising idea for real estate investment is to purchase a property with the goal of generating rental income or capital appreciation. This strategy involves acquiring a property and leveraging it to generate returns over time.

Investing in rental properties allows you to earn regular rental income, which can provide a steady cash flow and potentially cover mortgage payments and expenses. Additionally, properties in desirable locations may experience capital appreciation, leading to an increase in their market value over time.

To implement this idea successfully, it's important to carefully evaluate properties, assess rental demand in the area, and conduct thorough financial analysis to ensure the investment is financially viable. Additionally, being a responsible landlord and managing the property effectively are key factors in achieving success.

By purchasing a property for rental income or capital appreciation, you can create a source of passive income, build equity, and potentially benefit from property value appreciation in the long run. It's essential to conduct proper due diligence, consider market conditions, and seek professional advice to make informed investment decisions.

Risks: Economic Downturns, Property Market Fluctuations, Maintenance Costs

While investing in properties for rental income or capital appreciation can be lucrative, it's important to be aware of the associated risks. Here are some key risks to consider:

1. Economic Downturns: During economic downturns, rental demand may decrease, and property values can decline. This can impact rental income and the potential for capital appreciation.

2. Property Market Fluctuations: Real estate markets can experience fluctuations in supply and demand, which can affect property values. Market conditions, such as oversupply or changes in interest rates, can impact the profitability of the investment.

3. Maintenance Costs: Owning and maintaining a property comes with ongoing expenses, including repairs, maintenance, insurance, and property management fees. These costs can impact the profitability of the investment.

To mitigate these risks, it's important to conduct thorough market research, invest in locations with strong rental demand, maintain a financial buffer for unexpected expenses, and stay informed about economic trends and market conditions. Additionally, having a contingency plan and considering diversification within your real estate portfolio can help mitigate risks associated with individual properties.

By being aware of the risks and taking appropriate measures, investors can navigate challenges and optimize their real estate investment returns.

Time: Approximate Timeframe: 10-20 Years or More

Real estate investments are generally considered long-term investments with an approximate timeframe of 10-20 years or more. This extended time horizon allows investors to benefit from various factors that contribute to wealth creation in real estate.

Over time, properties tend to appreciate in value, especially in well-established and desirable locations. This appreciation is driven by factors such as population growth, urban development, and infrastructure improvements. Additionally, rental income can provide a consistent cash flow stream, which can further enhance the investment's returns.

The longer timeframe also allows investors to ride out market fluctuations and economic cycles, which can impact property values and rental demand in the short term. By maintaining a long-term perspective, investors can navigate through potential downturns and capitalize on the potential for growth over an extended period.

It's important to note that the specific timeframe for achieving significant returns may vary depending on factors such as the property's location, market conditions, and individual investment strategies. Patience, strategic planning, and diligent property management are key to realizing the full potential of real estate investments over the 10-20 year timeframe or beyond.

Conclusion

As we conclude this second book, "Unlocking the Potential: Real Estate Investments," in the series "From a Grand to a Million: The Secrets to Building Wealth," we reflect upon the invaluable knowledge gained and the transformative insights shared throughout our journey into the world of real estate investments.

In these pages, we explored the diverse opportunities that real estate presents for wealth creation. From understanding the various types of properties to grasping the intricacies of market trends, you have been equipped with the tools to make informed decisions in your investment journey.

Real estate investments are more than just financial transactions; they hold the potential to shape your future and create a lasting legacy. By diligently applying the strategies and principles outlined in this book, you are poised to unlock the doors to financial independence and security.

However, we also acknowledge that the path to success in real estate investments is not without its challenges. Market fluctuations, regulatory changes, and unforeseen circumstances may present hurdles along the way. Yet, armed with the knowledge gained, you are better prepared to navigate these obstacles with confidence and resilience.

We hope that the insights shared in this book have ignited your passion for real estate investments and inspired you to take actionable steps towards achieving your financial goals. Remember that building wealth through real estate is a journey that requires patience, perseverance, and continual learning.

As you venture forth in your wealth-building endeavors, keep in mind that each investment decision is an opportunity for growth and learning. Stay informed about market developments, seek guidance from experienced professionals, and adapt your strategies as needed.

On behalf of the entire "From a Grand to a Million" series, we thank you for joining us on this transformative journey. Whether you are just beginning your wealth-building path or have been on it for some time, remember that building wealth is a journey that extends beyond the boundaries of any single book.

As you continue to explore the world of wealth creation, be bold in your ambitions and relentless in your pursuit of financial prosperity. The secrets you have unlocked within these pages are a stepping stone towards a brighter future, where your dreams of financial freedom can become a reality.

May the knowledge gained from this book serve as a guiding light, propelling you towards a life filled with abundance, security, and the fulfillment of your deepest aspirations. As you embrace the potential of real estate investments, may you unlock doors to a future filled with endless opportunities.

Your journey towards building wealth has just begun, and we wish you all the success and fulfillment in the pursuit of your financial dreams.

www.ingramcontent.com/pod-product-compliance
Lightning Source LLC
Chambersburg PA
CBHW062353290526
45794CB00005B/2201